A Matter (

MW01673441

Murray Leinster

Alpha Editions

This edition published in 2022

ISBN : 9789356901711

Design and Setting By
Alpha Editions
www.alphaedis.com
Email - info@alphaedis.com

A MATTER OF IMPORTANCE

BY MURRAY LEINSTER

The importance of a matter is almost entirely a matter of your attitude. And whether you call something "a riot" or "a war" ... well, there is a difference, but what is it?

Nobody ever saw the message-torp. It wasn't to be expected. It came in on a course that extended backward to somewhere near the Rift—where there used to be Huks—and for a very, very long way it had traveled as only message-torps do travel. It hopped half a light-year in overdrive, and came back to normality long enough for its photocells to inspect the star-filled universe all about. Then it hopped another half light-year, and so on. For a long, long time it traveled in this jerky fashion.

Eventually, moving as it did in the straightest of straight lines, its photocells reported that it neared a star which had achieved first-magnitude brightness. It paused a little longer than usual while its action-circuits shifted. Then it swung to aim for the bright star, which was the sol-type sun Varenga. The torp sped toward it on a new schedule. Its overdrive hops dropped to light-month length. Its pauses in normality were longer. They lasted almost the fiftieth of a second.

When Varenga had reached a suitably greater brightness in the message-torp's estimation, it paused long enough to blast out its recorded message. It had been designed for this purpose and no other. Its overdrive hops shortened to one light-hour of distance covered. Regularly, its transmitter flung out a repetition of what it had been sent so far to say. In time it arrived within the limits of the Varenga system. Its hops diminished to light-minutes of distance only. It ceased to correct its course. It hurtled through the orbits of all the planets, uttering silently screamed duplicates of the broadcasts now left behind, to arrive later.

It did not fall into the sun, of course. The odds were infinitely against such a happening. It pounded past the sun, shrieking its news, and hurtled on out to the illimitable emptiness beyond. It was still squealing when it went out of human knowledge forever.

The state of things was routine. Sergeant Madden had the traffic desk that morning. He would reach retirement age in two more years, and it was a nagging reminder that he grew old. He didn't like it. There was another matter. His son Timmy had a girl, and she was on the way to Varenga IV on the *Cerberus*, and when she arrived Timmy would become a married man. Sergeant Madden contemplated this prospect. By the time his retirement came up, in the ordinary course of events he could very well be a grandfather. He was unable to imagine it. He rumbled to himself.

The telefax hummed and ejected a sheet of paper on top of other sheets in the desk's "In" cubicle. Sergeant Madden glanced absently at it. It was an operations-report sheet, to be referred to if necessary, but otherwise simply to be filed at the end of the day.

A voice crackled overhead.

"*Attention Traffic*," said the voice. "*The following report has been received and verified as off-planet. Message follows.*" That voice ceased and was replaced by another, which wavered and wabbled from the electron-spurts normal to solar systems and which make for auroras on planets. "*Mayday mayday mayday*," said the second voice. "*Call for help. Call for help. Ship* Cerberus *major breakdown overdrive heading Procyron III for refuge. Help urgently needed.*" There was a pause. "*Mayday mayday mayday. Call for help—*"

Sergeant Madden's face went blank. Timmy's girl was on the *Cerberus*. Then he growled and riffled swiftly through the operations-report sheets that had come in since his tour of duty began. He found the one he looked for. Yes. Patrolman Timothy Madden was now in overdrive in squad ship 740, delivering the monthly precinct report to Headquarters. He would be back in eight days. Maybe a trifle less, with his girl due to arrive on the *Cerberus* in nine and him to be married in ten. But—

Sergeant Madden swore. As a prospective bridegroom, Timmy's place was on this call for help to the *Cerberus*. But he wasn't available. It was in his line, because it was specifically a traffic job. The cops handled traffic, naturally, as they handled sanitary-code enforcement and delinks and mercantile offenses and murderers and swindlers and missing persons. Everything was dumped on the cops. They'd even handled the Huks in time gone by—which in still earlier times would have been called a space war and put down in all the history books. It was routine for the cops to handle the disabled or partly disabled *Cerberus*.

Sergeant Madden pushed a button marked "*Traffic Emergency*" and held it down until it lighted.

"You got that *Cerberus* report?" he demanded of the air about him.

"Just," said a voice overhead.

"What've you got on hand?" demanded Sergeant Madden.

"The *Aldeb*'s here," said the voice. "There's a minor overhaul going on, but we can get her going in six hours. She's slow, but you know her."

"Hm-m-m. Yeah," said Sergeant Madden. He added vexedly: "My son Timmy's girl is on board the *Cerberus*. He'll be wild he wasn't here. I'm going to take the ready squad ship and go on out. Passengers always fret when there's trouble and no cop around. Too bad Timmy's off on assignment."

"Yeah," said the Traffic Emergency voice. "Too bad. But we'll get the *Aldeb* off in six hours."

Sergeant Madden pushed another button. It lighted.

"Madden," he rumbled. "Desk. The *Cerberus*' had a breakdown. She's limpin' over to Procyron III for refuge to wait for help. The *Aldeb*'ll do the job on her, but I'm going to ride the squad ship out and make up the report. Who's next on call-duty?"

"Willis," said a crisp voice. "Squad ship 390. He's up for next call. Playing squint-eye in the squad room now."

"Pull him loose," Sergeant Madden ordered, "and send somebody to take the desk. Tell Willis I'll be on the tarmac in five minutes."

"Check," said the crisp voice.

Sergeant Madden lifted his thumb. All this was standard operational procedure. A man had the desk. An emergency call came in. That man took it and somebody else took the desk. Eminently fair. No favoritism; no throwing weight around; no glory-grabbing. Not that there was much glory in being a cop. But as long as a man was a cop, he was good. Sergeant Madden reflected with satisfaction that even if he was getting on to retirement age, he was still a cop.

He made two more calls. One was to Records for the customary full information on the *Cerberus* and on the Procyron system. The other was to the flat where Timmy lived with him. It was going to be lonely when Timmy got married and had a home of his own. Sergeant Madden dialed for message-recording and gruffly left word for Timmy. He, Timmy's father, was going on ahead to make the report on the *Cerberus*. Timmy wasn't to worry. The ship might be a few days late, but Timmy'd better make the most of them. He'd be married a long time!

Sergeant Madden got up, grunting, from his chair. Somebody came in to take over the desk. Sergeant Madden nodded and waved his hand. He went out and took the slide-stair down to the tarmac where squad ship 390 waited in standard police readiness. Patrolman Willis arrived at the stubby little craft seconds after the sergeant.

"Procyron III," said Sergeant Madden, rumbling. "I figure three days. You told your wife?"

"I called," said Patrolman Willis resignedly.

They climbed into the squad ship. Police ships, naturally, had their special drive, which could lift them off without rocket aid and gave them plenty of speed, but filled up the hull with so much machinery that it was only practical for such ships. Commercial craft were satisfied with low-power drives, which meant that spaceport facilities lifted them to space and pulled them down again. They carried rockets for emergency landing, but the main thing was that they had a profitable pay load. Squad ships didn't carry anything but two men and their equipment.

Sergeant Madden dogged the door shut. The ship fell up toward the sky. The heavens became that blackness-studded-with-jewels which is space. A great yellow sun flared astern. A half-bright, half-dark globe lay below-the planet Varenga IV, on which the precinct police station for this part of the galaxy had its location.

Patrolman Willis, frowning with care, established the squad ship's direction, while Sergeant Madden observed without seeming to do so. Presently Patrolman Willis pushed a button. The squad ship went into overdrive.

It was perfectly commonplace in all its aspects.

The galaxy went about its business. Stars shone, and planets moved around them, and double stars circled each other like waltzing couples. There were also comets and meteors and calcium-clouds and high-energy free nuclei, all of which acted as was appropriate for them. On some millions of planets winds blew and various organisms practiced photosynthesis. Waves ran across seas. Clouds formed and poured down rain. On the relatively small number of worlds so far inhabited by humans, people went about their business with no thought for such things or anything not immediately affecting their lives. And the cops went about their business.

Sergeant Madden dozed most of the first day of overdrive travel. He had nothing urgent to do, as yet. This was only a routine trip. The *Cerberus* had had a breakdown in her overdrive. Commercial ships' drives being what they were, it meant that on her emergency drive she could only limp along at maybe eight or ten lights. Which meant years to port, with neither food nor air for the journey. But it was not even conceivable to rendezvous with a rescue ship in the emptiness between stars. So the *Cerberus* had sent a message-torp and was crawling to a refuge-planet, more or less surveyed a hundred years before. There she would land by emergency rockets, because her drive couldn't take the strain. Once aground, the *Cerberus* should wait for help. There was nothing else to be done. But everything was nicely in hand. The squad ship headed briskly for the planet Procyron III, and Sergeant Madden would take the data for a proper, official, emergency-call traffic report on the incident, and in time the *Aldeb* would turn up and make emergency repairs and see the *Cerberus* out to space again and headed for port once more.

This was absolutely all that there was to anticipate. Traffic handled such events as a matter of course. So Sergeant Madden dozed during most of the first day of overdrive. He reflected somnolently when awake that it was fitting for Timmy's father to be on the job when Timmy's girl was in difficulty, since Timmy was off somewhere else.

On the second day he conversed more or less with Patrolman Willis. Willis was a young cop, almost as young as Timmy. He took himself very seriously. When Sergeant Madden reached for the briefing-data, he found it disturbed. Willis had read up on the kind of ship the *Cerberus* was, and on the characteristics of Procyron III as recorded a century before. The *Cerberus* was a semi-freighter, Candless type. Procyron III was a water-planet with less than ten per cent of land. Which was unfortunate, because its average temperature and orbit made it highly suitable for human occupation. Had the ten per cent of solid ground been in one piece, it would doubtless have been colonized. But the ground was an archipelago.

"Hm-m-m," said Sergeant Madden, after reading. "The survey recommends this northern island for emergency landing. Eh?"

Willis nodded. "Huks used to use it. Not the island. The planet."

Sergeant Madden yawned. It seemed pathetic to him that young cops like Willis and even Timmy referred so often to Huks. There weren't any, any more. Being a cop meant carrying out purely routine tasks, nowadays. They were important tasks, of course. Without the cops, there couldn't be any civilization. But Willis and Timmy didn't think of it that way. Not yet. To them being a cop was still a matter of glamour rather than routine. They probably even regretted the absence of Huks. But when a man reached Sergeant Madden's age, glamour didn't matter. He had to remember that his job was worth doing, in itself.

"Yeah," said Sergeant Madden. "There was quite a time with those Huks."

"Did you ... did you ever see a Huk, sir?" asked Willis.

"Before my time," said Sergeant Madden. "But I've talked to men who worked on the case."

It did not occur to him that the Huks would hardly have been called a "case" by anybody but a cop. When human colonies spread through this sector, they encountered an alien civilization. By old-time standards, it was quite a culture. The Huks had a good technology, they had spaceships, and they were just beginning to expand, themselves, from their own home planet or planets. If they'd had a few more centuries of development, they might have been a menace to humanity. But the humans got started first.

There being no longer any armies or navies when the Huks were discovered, the matter of intelligent nonhumans was a matter for the cops. So the police matter-of-factly tried to incorporate the Huk culture into the human. They explained the rules by which human civilization worked. They painstakingly tried to arrange a sub-precinct station on the largest Huk home planet, with Huk cops in charge. They made it clear that they had nothing to do with politics and were simply concerned with protecting civilized people from those in their midst who didn't want to be civilized.

The Huks wouldn't have it. They bristled, proudly. They were defiant. They considered themselves not only as good as humans—the cops didn't care what they thought—but they insisted on acting as if they were better.

They reacted, in fact, as humans would have done if just at the beginning of their conquest of the stars, they'd run into an expanding, farther-advanced race which tried to tell them what they had to do. The Huks fought.

"They fought pretty good," said Sergeant Madden tolerantly. "Not killer-fashion—like delinks. The Force had to give 'em the choice of joining up or getting out. Took years to get 'em out. Had to use all the off-duty men from six precincts to handle the last riot."

The conflict he called a riot would have been termed a space battle by a navy or an army. But the cops operated within a strictly police frame of reference, which was the reverse of military. They weren't trying to subjugate the Huks, but to make them behave. In consequence, their tactics were unfathomable to the Huks—who thought in military terms. Squadrons of police ships which would have seemed ridiculous to a fighting-force commander threw the Huks off-balance, kept them off-balance, did a scrupulous minimum of damage to them, and thereby kept out of every trap the Huks set for them. In the end the cops supervised and assisted at the embittered, rebellious emigration of a race. The Huks took off for the far side of the galaxy. They'd neither been conquered nor exterminated. But Sergeant Madden thought of the decisive fracas as a riot rather than a battle.

"Yeah," he repeated. "They acted a lot like delinks."

Patrolman Willis spoke with some heat about delinks, who are the bane of all police forces everywhere. They practice adolescent behavior even after they grow up—but they never grow up. It is delinks who put stink-bombs in public places and write threatening letters and give warnings of bombs about to go off—and sometimes set them—and stuff dirt into cold rocket-nozzles and sometimes kill people and go incontinently hysterical because they didn't mean to. Delinks do most of the damaging things that have no sense to them. There is no cop who has not wanted to kill some grinning, half-scared, half-defiant delink who hasn't yet realized that he's destroyed half a million credits' worth of property or crippled somebody for life—for no reason at all.

Sergeant Madden listened to the denunciation of all the delink tribe. Then he yawned again.

"I know!" he said. "I don't like 'em either. But we got 'em. We always will have 'em. Like old age."

Then he made computations with a stubby pencil and asked reflectively:

"When're you coming out of overdrive?"

Patrolman Willis told him. Sergeant Madden nodded.

"I'll take another nap," he observed. "We'll be there a good twenty-two hours before the *Aldeb.*"

The little squad ship went on at an improbable multiple of the speed of light. After all, this was a perfectly normal performance. Just an ordinary bit of business for the cops.

Sergeant Madden belched when the squad ship came out of overdrive. He watched with seeming indifference while Patrolman Willis took a spectro on the star ahead and to the left, and painstakingly compared the reading with the ancient survey-data on the Procyron system. It had to match, of course, unless there'd been extraordinarily bad astrogation.

Willis put the spectroscope away, estimated for himself, and then checked with the dial that indicated the brightness of the still point-sized star. He said:

"Four light-weeks, I make it."

Sergeant Madden nodded. A superior officer should never do anything useful, so long as a subordinate isn't making a serious mistake. That is the way subordinates are trained to become superiors, in time. Patrolman Willis set a time-switch and pushed the overdrive button. The squad ship hopped, and abruptly the local sun had a perceptible disk. Willis made the usual tests for direction of rotation, to get the ecliptic plane. He began to search for planets. As he found them, he checked with the reference data. All this was tedious. Sergeant Madden grunted:

"That'll be it," he said, and pointed. "Water world. It's the color of ocean. Try it."

Patrolman Willis threw on the telescope screen. The image of the distant planet leaped into view. It was Procyron III. The spiral cloud-arms of a considerable storm showed in the southern hemisphere, but in the north there was a group or specks which would be the planet's only solid ground—the archipelago reported by the century-old survey. The *Cerberus* should have been the first ship to land there in a hundred years, and the squad ship should be the second.

Patrolman Willis got the squad ship competently over to the planet, a diameter out. He juggled to position over the archipelago. Sergeant Madden turned on the space phone. Nothing. He frowned. A grounded ship awaiting help should transmit a beam signal to guide its rescuer. But nothing came up from the ground.

Patrolman Willis looked at him uncertainly. Sergeant Madden rumbled and swung the telescope below. The surface of the planet appeared—deep water, practically black beneath a surface reflection of daytime sky. The image shifted—a patch of barren rocks. The sergeant glanced at the survey picture, shifted the telescope, and found the northern-most island. He swelled the picture. He could see the white of monstrous surf breaking on the windward shore—waves that had gathered height going all around the planet. He traced the shoreline. There was a bay up at the top.

He centered the shoreline of the bay and put on maximum magnification. Then he pointed a stubby forefinger. A singular, perfectly straight streak of black appeared, beginning a little distance inland from the bay and running up into what appeared to be higher ground. The streak ended not far from a serpentine arm of the sea which almost cut the island in half.

"That'll be it," said Sergeant Madden, rumbling. "The *Cerberus* had to land on her rockets. She had some ground speed. She burned a ten-mile streak on the ground, coming down." He growled. "Commercial skippers! Should've matched velocity aloft! Take her down."

The squad ship drove for ground.

Patrolman Willis steadied the ship no more than a few thousand feet high, above the streak of scorched ground and ashes.

"It was heading inland, all right," rumbled Sergeant Madden. "Lucky! If it'd been heading the other way, it could've gone out and landed in the sea. That would ha' been a mess! But where is it?"

The squad ship descended farther. It followed the lane of carbonized soil. That marking narrowed—the *Cerberus* had plainly been descending. Then the streak came to an end. It pinched out to nothing. The *Cerberus* should have been at its end.

It wasn't. There was no ship down on Procyron III.

The matter ceased to be routine. If the liner's drive conked out where Procyron III was the nearest refuge planet, it should have landed here at least six days ago. Some ship had landed here recently.

"Set down," grunted Sergeant Madden.

Patrolman Willis obeyed. The squad ship came to rest in a minor valley, a few hundred yards from the end of the rocket-blast trail. Sergeant Madden got out. Patrolman Willis followed him. This was a duly surveyed and recommended refuge planet. There was no need to check the air or take precautions against inimical animal or vegetable life. The planet was safe.

They clambered over small rocky obstacles until they came to the end of the scorched line. They surveyed the state of things in silence.

A ship had landed here recently. Its blue-white rocket flames had melted gulleys in the soil, turned it to slag, and then flung silky, gossamer threads of slag-wool over the rocks nearby.

At the end of the melted-away hollows, twin slag-lined holes went down deep into the ground. They were take-off holes. Rockets had burned them deeply as they gathered force to lift the ship away again.

Sergeant Madden scrambled to the edge of the nearest blast-well. He put his hand on the now-solidified, glassy slag. It wasn't warm, but it wasn't cold. The glass-lined hole a rocket leaves takes a long time to cool down.

"She landed here, all right," he grunted. "But she took off again before the torp arrived to tell us about it."

Willis protested:

"But, sergeant! She only had one set of rockets! She couldn't have taken off again! She didn't have the rockets to do it with!"

"I know she couldn't," growled the sergeant. "But she did."

The *Cerberus*, once landed, should have waited here. It was not only a police regulation; it was common sense. When a ship broke down in space, the exclusive hope for that ship's company lay in a refuge planet for ships in that traffic lane. Even lifeboats could ordinarily reach some refuge planet, for picking up later. They couldn't possibly be located otherwise. With three dimensions in which to be missed, and light-years of distance in which to miss them—no ship or boat had ever been found as much as a light-week out in space. No ship with a crippled drive could possibly be helped unless it got to a specified refuge world where it could be found. No ship which had reached a refuge planet could conceivably want to leave it.

There was also the fact that no ship which had made such a landing would have extra rockets with which to take off for departure.

The *Cerberus* had landed. Timmy's girl was on it. It had taken off again. It was either an impossible mass suicide or something worse. It certainly wasn't routine.

Patrolman Willis asked hesitantly:

"D'you think, sergeant, it could be Huks sneaked back—?"

Sergeant Madden did not answer. He went back to the squad ship and armed himself. Patrolman Willis followed suit. The sergeant boobied the squad ship so no unauthorized person could make use of it, and so it would disable itself if anyone with expert knowledge tried. Therefore, nobody with expert knowledge would try.

The two cops began a painstaking quest for police-type evidence to tell them what had happened, and how and why the *Cerberus* was missing, after a clumsy but safe landing on Procyron III and when all sanity demanded that it stay there, and when it was starkly impossible for it to leave.

Sergeant Madden and Patrolman Willis were, self-evidently, the only human beings on a planet some nine thousand miles in diameter. It was easy to compute that the nearest other humans would be at least some thousands of thousands of millions of miles away—so far away that distance had no meaning. This planet was something over nine-tenth rolling sea, but there were a few tens of thousands of square miles of solid ground in the one archipelago that broke the ocean's surface. It was such loneliness as very few people ever experience. But they did not notice it. They were busy.

They went over the ground immediately about the landing place. Rocket flame had splashed it, both at the *Cerberus'* landing and at the impossible take-off. There was nothing within a hundred yards not burned to a crisp. They searched outside that area. Sergeant Madden rumbled to his companion:

"Where'd the other ship land?"

Patrolman Willis blinked at him.

"There had to be another ship!" said Sergeant Madden irritably. "To bring the extra rockets. The other ship had to've brought 'em. And it had to have rockets of its own. There's no spaceport here!"

Patrolman Willis blinked again. Then he saw. The *Cerberus* carried one set of emergency-landing rockets, for use in a descent on a refuge planet if the need arose. The need had arisen and the *Cerberus* had used them. Then, from somewhere, another set of rockets had been produced for it to use in leaving. Those other rockets must have come on another ship. But it was a trifle more complicated than that. The *Cerberus* had carried one set of rockets and used them. One. It had been supplied with another set from somewhere. Two. They must have been brought by a ship which also used a set of rockets to land by. That made three. Then the other ship must have had a fourth set for its own take-off, or it would be grounded forever on Procyron III.

Patrolman Willis frowned.

"We looked pretty carefully from aloft," he said uncomfortably. "If there'd been another burned-off landing place, we'd have seen it."

"I know," rumbled Sergeant Madden. "And we didn't. But there must've been another ship aground when the *Cerberus* came in. Where was it? It prob'ly knew the *Cerberus* was landing to wait for help. How? If somebody was coming to help the *Cerberus* it would be bound to spot the other ship, and it didn't want to be spotted. Why? Anyhow, it must've taken the *Cerberus* and sent it off, and then taken off itself, leaving nothing sensible for us to think. 'Sounds like delinks." Then he growled. "Only it's not. There'd have to be too many men. Delinks don't work together more'n two or three. Too jealous of showin' off. But where was that other ship, and what was it doin' here?"

Patrolman Willis hesitated, and then said:

"There used to be pirates, sergeant."

"Uh-huh," said the sergeant. "You had it right the first time, most likely. Not delinks. Not pirates. You said Huks." He looked around, estimatingly. "The rockets had to be brought here from somewhere else where they'd been landed. I'm betting the tracks were covered pretty careful. But rockets are heavy. Manhandlin' them, whoever was doin' it would take the easiest way. Hm-m-m. There's water close by over yonder. Sort of a sound in there—too narrow to be a bay. Let's have a look. And the slopes are easiest that way, too."

He led off to the eastward. He thought of Timmy's girl. He'd never seen her, but Timmy was going to marry her. She was on the *Cerberus*. It was the job of the cops to take care of whatever dilemma that ship might be in. As of here and now, it was Sergeant Madden's job. But besides that, he thought of the way Timmy would feel if anything happened to the girl he meant to marry. As Timmy's father, the sergeant had to do something. He wanted to do it fast. But it had to be done the right way.

The route he chose was rocky, but it was nearly the only practicable route away from the burned-dead landing place. He climbed toward what on this planet was the east. There were pinnacles and small precipices. There were small, fleshy-leaved bushes growing out of such tiny collections of soil as had formed in cracks and crevices in the rock.

Sergeant Madden noted that one such bush was wilted. He stopped. He bent over and carefully felt of the stones about it. A small rock came out. The bush had been out of the ground before. It had carefully been replaced. By someone.

"The rockets came this way," said the sergeant, with finality. "Hauled over this pass to the *Cerberus*. Somebody must've knocked this bush loose while workin' at getting 'em along. So he replanted it. Only not good enough. It wilted."

"Who did it?" demanded Patrolman Willis.

"Who we want to know about," growled Sergeant Madden. "Maybe Huks. Come on!"

He scrambled ahead. He wheezed as he climbed and descended. After half a mile, Patrolman Willis said abruptly:

"You figure they all left, before anybody tried to find 'em?"

The sergeant grunted affirmatively. A quarter mile still farther, the rocky ground fell away. There was the gleam of water below them. Rocky cliffs enclosed an arm of the sea that came deep into the land, here. In the cliffs rock-strata tilted insanely. There were red and yellow and black layers—mostly yellow and black. They showed in startlingly clear contrast.

"Right!" said Sergeant Madden in morose satisfaction. "I thought there might've been a boat. But this's it!"

He went down a steep descent to the very edge of the sound—it was even more like a fjord—where the waters of the ocean came in among the island's hills. On the far side, a little cascade leaped and bubbled down to join the sea.

"You go that way," commanded Sergeant Madden, "and I'll go this. We've got two things to look for—a shallow place in the water coming right up to shore. And look for signs of traffic from the cliffs to the water. By the color of those rocks, we'd ought to find both."

He lumbered away along the water's edge. There were no creatures which sang or chirped. The only sounds were wind and the lapping of waves against the shore. It was very, very lonely.

Half a mile from the point of his first descent, the sergeant found a shoal. It was a flat space of shallow water—discoverable by the color of the bottom. The water was not over four feet deep. It was a remarkably level shoal place.

He whistled on his fingers. When Patrolman Willis reached him, he pointed to the cliffs directly across the beach from the shallow water. Lurid yellow tints stained the cliff walls. Odd masses of fallen stone dotted the cliff foot. At one place they were piled high. That pile looked quite natural—except that it was at the very center of the shore line next the shoal.

"This rock's yellow," said Sergeant Madden, rumbling a little. "It's mineral. If we had a Geiger, it'd be raising hell, here. There's a mine in there. Uranium. If a ship came down on rockets, an' landed in that shoal place yonder ... why ... it wouldn't leave a burned spot comin' down or takin' off, either. Y'see?"

Patrolman Willis said: "Look here, sergeant—"

"I'm in command here," growled Sergeant Madden. "Huks didn't booby trap. Proud as hell, and touchy as all get-out, but not killers. Not crazy killers, anyhow. You go get up yonder. Up where we started down. Then go on away. Back to the squad ship. If I don't come along, anyhow you'll know what's what when the *Aldeb* comes."

Patrolman Willis expostulated. Sergeant Madden was firm. In the end, Patrolman Willis went away. And Sergeant Madden sat at ease and rested until he had time enough to get back to the squad ship. It was true that the Huks didn't booby trap. They hadn't had the practice, anyhow, eighty years ago. But this was a very important matter. Maybe they considered it so important that they'd changed their policy concerning this.

Wheezing a little, Sergeant Madden pulled away large stones and small ones. An opening appeared behind them. He grunted and continued his labor. Nothing happened. The mouth of a mine shaft appeared, going horizontally into the cliff.

Puffing from his exertions, Sergeant Madden went in. It was necessary if he were to make a routine examination.

The *Aldeb* came in a full day later. It descended, following the space beacon the squad ship sent up from its resting place. The *Aldeb* was not an impressive sight, of course. It was a medium-sized police salvage ship. It had a crew of fifteen, and it was powerfully engined, and it contained a respectable amount of engineering experience and ability, plus some spare parts and, much more important, the tools with which to make others. It came down in a highly matter-of-fact fashion, and Sergeant Madden and Patrolman Willis went over to it to explain the situation.

"The *Cerberus* came in on rockets," rumbled the sergeant, in the salvage ship's skipper's cabin. "She landed. We found signs that some of her people came out an' strolled around lookin' for souvenirs and such. I make a guess that there was a minin' man among them, but it's only a guess. Anyhow somebody went over to where there's some parti-colored cliffs, where the sea comes away inland. And when they got to that place ... why ... there was a ship there. Then."

He paused, frowning.

"It would've been standing on an artificial shoal place, about thirty yards from a shaft that was the mouth of a mine. Uranium. And there's been a lot of uranium taken outta there! It was hauled right outta the mine shaft across the beach to the ship that was waitin'. And there's fresh work in that mine, but not a tool or a scrap of paper to tell who was workin' it. It must've been cleaned up like that every time a ship left after loadin' up. Humans wouldn't've done it. They wouldn't care. Huks would. There's not supposed to be any of them left in these parts, but I'm guessing the mine was dug by Huks, and the *Cerberus* was taken away by them because the humans on the *Cerberus* found out there was Huks around."

Patrolman Willis said: "The sergeant took a chance on the mine being booby-trapped and went in, after sending me out of range."

The sergeant scowled at him and went on.

"How it happened don't matter. Maybe somebody spotted the ship from the *Cerberus* as it was comin' down. Maybe anything. But whoever run the mine found out somebody knew they were there, so they rushed the *Cerberus*—there prob'ly wasn't even a stun-pistol on board to fight with—and they put new rockets on her."

The skipper of the salvage ship *Aldeb* nodded wisely.

"A ship comin' to load up minerals where there wasn't any spaceport," he observed, "would have a set of rockets to land on, empty, and a double set to take off on, loaded. Yeah."

"They must've figured," said Sergeant Madden, "that we just couldn't make any sense out of what we found. And if we hadn't turned up that mine, maybe never would. But anyhow they sent the *Cerberus* off and covered everything up and went off to stay, themselves, until we gave up and went home."

"I wonder," said the skipper of the *Aldeb*, "where they took the *Cerberus*? That's my job!"

"Not far," grunted Sergeant Madden. "They had to be taking the *Cerberus* somewhere. If they just wanted to wipe it out, after they rushed it, they coulda just set off its fuel like it'd happened in a bad landing. And that landing was bad! If there'd been a fuel-explosion crater at the end of that burnt line on the ground, nobody'd ever've looked further. But there wasn't. So there's a place they're takin' the *Cerberus* to. But it's got a brokedown drive. It can only hobble along. They can't try to get but so far! What's the nearest sol-type star?"

The *Aldeb*'s skipper pushed a button and the Precinct Atlas came out of its slot. The skipper punched keys and the atlas clicked and whirred. Then its screen lighted. It showed a report on a solar system that had been fully surveyed.

"Uh-uh," grunted the sergeant. "A survey woulda showed up if a planet was Huk-occupied. What's next nearest?"

Again the atlas whirred and clicked. A single line of type appeared. It said, "*Sirene, 1432. Unsurveyed.*" The galactic co-ordinates followed. That was all.

"This looks likely!" said the sergeant. "Unsurveyed, and off the ship lanes. It ain't between any place and any other. It could go a thousand years and never be landed on. It's got planets."

It was highly logical. According to Krishnamurti's Law, any sol-type sun was bound to have planets of such-and-such relative sizes in orbits of such-and-such relative distances.

"Willis and me," said the sergeant, "we'll go over and see if there's Huks there and if they've got the *Cerberus*. You better get this stuff on a message-torp ready to send off if you have to. Are you going to come over to this—Sirene 1432?"

The skipper of the *Aldeb* shrugged.

"Might as well. Why go home and have to come back again? There could be a lot of Huks there."

"Yeah," admitted Sergeant Madden. "I'd guess a whole planet full of 'em that laid low when the rest were scrapping with the Force. The others lost and went clean across the galaxy. These characters stayed close. I'm guessing. But they hid their mine, here. They could've been stewing in their own juice these past eighty years, getting set to put up a hell of a scrap when somebody found 'em. We'll be the ones to do it."

He stood up and shook himself.

"It's not far," he repeated. "Our boat's just fast enough we ought to get there a couple of days after the *Cerberus* sets down. You'd ought to be five-six hours behind us." He considered. "Meet you north pole farthest planet out this side of the sun. Right?"

"I'll look for you there," said the skipper of the *Aldeb.*

Sergeant Madden and Patrolman Willis went out of the salvage ship and trudged to the squad ship. They climbed in.

"You got the co-ordinates?" asked the sergeant.

"I copied them off the atlas," said Willis.

Sergeant Madden settled himself comfortably.

"We'll go over," he grumbled, "and see what makes these Huks tick. They raised a lot of hell, eighty years ago. It took all the off-duty men from six precincts to handle the last riot. The Huks had got together and built themselves a fightin' fleet then, though. It's not likely there's more than one planetful of them where we're going. I thought they'd all been moved out."

He shook his head vexedly.

"No need for 'em to have to go, except they wouldn't play along with humans. Acted like delinks, they did. Only proud. Y'don't get mad fighting 'em. So I heard, anyway. If they only had sense you could get along with them."

He dogged the door shut. Patrolman Willis pushed a button. The squad ship fell toward the sky.

Very matter-of-factly.

On the way over, in overdrive, Sergeant Madden again dozed a great deal of the time. Sergeants do not fraternize extensively with mere patrolmen, even on assignments. Especially not very senior sergeants only two years from retirement. Patrolman Willis met with the sergeant's approval, to be sure. Timmy was undoubtedly more competent as a cop, but Timmy would have been in a highly emotional state with his girl on the *Cerberus* and that ship in the hands of the Huks.

Between naps, the sergeant somnolently went over what he knew about the alien race. He'd heard that their thumbs were on the outside of their hands. Intelligent nonhumans would have to have hands, and with some equivalent of opposable thumbs, if their intelligence was to be of any use to them. They pretty well had to be bipeds, too, and if they weren't warm-blooded they couldn't have the oxygen-supply that highgrade brain cells require.

There were even certain necessary psychological facts. They had to be capable of learning and of passing on what they'd learned, or they'd never have gotten past an instinctual social system. To pass on acquired knowledge, they had to have family units in which teaching was done to the young—at least at the beginning. Schools might have been invented later. Most of all, their minds had to work logically to cope with a logically constructed universe. In fact, they had to be very much like humans, in almost all significant respects, in order to build up a civilization and develop sciences and splendidly to invade space just a few centuries before humans found them.

But, said Sergeant Madden to himself, *I bet they've still got armies and navies!*

Patrolman Willis looked at him inquiringly, but the sergeant scowled at his own thoughts. Yet the idea was very likely. When Huks first encountered humans, they bristled with suspicion. They were definitely on the defensive when they learned that humans had been in space longer—much longer—than they had, and already occupied planets in almost fifteen per cent of the galaxy.

Sergeant Madden found his mind obscurely switching to the matter of delinks—those characters who act like adolescents, not only while they are kids, but after. They were the permanent major annoyance of the cops, because what they did didn't make sense. Learned books explained why people went delink, of course. Mostly it was that they were madly ambitious to be significant, to matter in some fashion, and didn't have the ability to matter in the only ways they could understand. They wanted to drive themselves to eminence, and frantically snatched at chances to make themselves nuisances because they couldn't wait to be important any other way.

Sergeant Madden blinked slowly to himself. When humans first took to space a lot of them were after glamour, which is the seeming of importance. His son Timmy was on the cops because he thought it glamorous. Patrolman Willis was probably the same way. Glamour is the offer of importance. An offer of importance is glamour.

The sergeant grunted to himself. A possible course of action came into his mind. He and Patrolman Willis were on the way to the solar system Sirene 1432, where Krishnamurti's Law said there ought to be something very close to a terran-type planet in either the third or fourth orbit out from the sun. That planet would be inhabited by Huks, who were very much like humans. They knew of the defeat and forced emigration of their fellow-Huks in other solar systems. They'd hidden from humans—and it must have outraged their pride. So they must be ready to put up a desperate and fanatical fight if they were ever discovered.

A squad ship with two cops in it, and a dumpy salvage ship with fifteen more, did not make an impressive force to try to deal with a planetary population which bitterly hated humans. But the cops did not plan conquest. They were neither a fighting rescue expedition nor a punitive one. They were simply cops on assignment to get the semi-freighter *Cerberus* back in shape to travel on her lawful occasions among the stars, and to see that she and her passengers and crew got to the destination for which they'd started. The cop's purpose was essentially routine. And the Huks couldn't possibly imagine it.

Sergeant Madden settled some things in his mind and dozed off again.

When the squad ship came out of overdrive and he was awakened by the unpleasantness of breakout, he yawned. He looked on without comment as Patrolman Willis matter-of-factly performed the tricky task of determining the ecliptic while a solar system's sun was little more than a first-magnitude star. It was wholly improbable that anything like Huk patrol ships would be out so far. It was even more improbable that any kind of detection devices would be in operation. Any approaching ship could travel several times as fast as any signal.

Patrolman Willis searched painstakingly. He found a planet which was a mere frozen lump of matter in vastness. It was white from a layer of frozen gases piled upon its more solid core. He made observations.

"I can find it again, sir, to meet the *Aldeb*. Orders, sir?"

"Orders?" demanded Sergeant Madden. "What? Oh. Head in toward the sun. The Huks'll be on Planet Three or Four, most likely. And that's where they'll have the *Cerberus*."

The squad ship continued sunward while Patrolman Willis continued his observations. A star-picture along the ecliptic. An hour's run on interplanetary drive—no overdrive field in use. Another picture. The two prints had only to be compared with a blinker for planets to stick out like sore thumbs, as contrasted with stars that showed no parallax. Sirene I—the innermost planet—was plainly close to a transit. II was away on the far side of its orbit. III was also on the far side. IV was in quadrature. There was the usual gap where V should have been. VI—it didn't matter. They'd passed VIII a little while since, a ball of stone with a frigid gas-ice covering.

Patrolman Willis worked painstakingly with amplifiers on what oddments could be picked up in space.

"It's Four, sir," he reported unnecessarily, because the sergeant had watched as he worked. "They've got detectors out. I could just barely pick up the pulses. But by the time they've been reflected back they'll be away below thermal noise-volume. I don't think even multiples could pick 'em out. I'm saying, sir, that I don't think they can detect us at this distance."

Sergeant Madden grunted.

"D'you think we came this far not to be noticed?" he asked. But he was not peevish. Rather, he seemed more thoroughly awake than he'd been since the squad ship left the Precinct substation back on Varenga IV. He rubbed his hands a little and stood up. "Hold it a minute, Willis."

He went back to the auxiliary-equipment locker. He returned to his seat beside Patrolman Willis. He opened the breech of the ejector-tube beside his chair.

"You've had street-fighting training," he said almost affably, "at the Police Academy. And siege-of-criminals courses too, eh?" He did not wait for an answer. "It's historic," he observed, "that since time began cops've been stickin' out hats for crooks to shoot at, and that crooks've been shooting, thinking there were heads in 'em."

He put a small object in the ejector tube, poked it to proper seating, and settled himself comfortably, again.

"Can you make it to about a quarter-million miles of Four," he asked cheerfully, "in one hop?"

Patrolman Willis set up the hop-timer. Sergeant Madden was pleased that he aimed the squad ship not exactly at the minute disk which was Planet IV of this system. It was prudence against the possibility of an error in the reading of distance.

"Ever use a marker, Willis?"

Patrolman Willis said: "No, sir."

Before he'd finished saying it the squad ship had hopped into overdrive and out again.

Sergeant Madden approved of the job. His son Timmy couldn't have done better. Here was Planet IV before them, a little off to one side, as was proper. They had run no risk of hitting in overdrive.

The distance was just about a quarter-million miles, if Krishnamurti's Law predicting the size and distance of planets in a sol-type system was reliable. The world was green and had icecaps. There should always be, in a system of this kind, at least one oxygen-planet with a nearly-terran-normal range of temperature. That usually meant green plants and an ocean or two. There wasn't quite as much sea as usual, on this planet, and therefore there were some extensive yellow areas that must be desert. But it was a good, habitable world. Anybody whose home it was would defend it fiercely.

"Hm-m-m," said Sergeant Madden. He took the ejector-tube lanyard in his hand. He computed mentally. About a quarter-million miles, say. A second and a half to alarm, down below. Five seconds more to verification. Another five to believe it. Not less than twenty altogether to report and get authority to fire. The Huks were a fighting race and presumably organized, so they'd have a chain of command and decisions would be made at the top. Army stuff, or navy. Not like the cops, where everybody knew both the immediate and final purposes of any operation in progress, and could act without waiting for orders.

It should be not less than thirty seconds before a firing key made contact down below. As a matter of history, years ago the Huks had used eighty-gravity rockets with tracking-heads and bust-bombs on them. These Huks would hardly be behind the others in equipment. And back then, too, Huks kept their rocket missiles out in orbit where they could flare into eighty-gee acceleration without wasting time getting out to where an enemy was. In their struggle against the cops two generations ago the Huks had had to learn that fighting wasn't all drama and heroics. The cops had taken the glamour out when they won. So the Huks wouldn't waste time making fine gestures now. The squad ship had appeared off their planet. It had not transmitted a code identification-signal the instant it came out of overdrive. The Huks were hiding from the cops, so they'd shoot.

"Hop on past," commanded Sergeant Madden, "the instant I jerk the ejector lanyard. Don't fool around. Over the pole will do."

Patrolman Willis set the hop-timer. Twenty seconds. Twenty-two. Three. Four.

"Hop!" said Sergeant Madden. As he spoke, he jerked the lanyard.

Before the syllable was finished, Patrolman Willis pressed hard on the overdrive button. There came the always-nauseating sensation of going into overdrive combined with the even more unpleasant sensation of coming out of it. The squad ship was somewhere else.

A vast, curving whiteness hung catercornered in the sky. It was the planet's icecap, upside down. Patrolman Willis had possibly cut it a trifle too fine.

"Right," said the sergeant comfortably. "Now swing about to go back and meet the *Aldeb.* But wait."

The stars and the monstrous white bowl reeled in their positions as the ship turned. Sergeant Madden felt that he could spare seconds, here. He ignored the polar regions of Sirene IV, hanging upside down to rearward from the squad ship. Even a planetary alarm wouldn't get polar-area observers set to fire in much less than forty seconds, and there'd have to be some lag in response to instrument reports. It wouldn't be as if trouble had been anticipated at just this time.

The squad ship steadied. Sergeant Madden looked with pleasurable anticipation back to where the ship had come out of overdrive and lingered for twenty-four seconds. Willis had moved the squad ship from that position, but the sergeant had left a substitute. The small object he'd dropped from the ejector tube now swelled and writhed and struggled. In pure emptiness, a shape of metal foil inflated itself. It was surprisingly large—almost the size of the squad ship. But in emptiness the fraction of a cubic inch of normal-pressure gas would inflate a foil bag against no resistance at all. This flimsy shape even jerked into motion. Released gas poured out its back. There was no resistance to acceleration save mass, which was negligible.

A sudden swirling cloud of vapor appeared where the squad ship's substitute went mindlessly on its way. The vapor rushed toward the space-marker.

A star appeared. It was a strictly temporary star, but even from a quarter-million-mile distance it was incredibly bright. It was a bomb, blasting a metal-foil flimsy which the electronic brain of a missile-rocket could only perceive as an unidentified and hence enemy object. Bomb and rocket and flimsy metal foil turned together to radioactive metal vapor.

Sergeant Madden knew professional admiration.

"Thirty-four seconds!" he said approvingly.

The Huks could not have expected the appearance of an enemy just here and now. It was the first such appearance in all the planet's history. They certainly looked for no consequences of the seizure of the *Cerberus*, carefully managed as that had been. So to detonate a bomb against an unexpected inimical object within thirty-four seconds after its appearance was very good work indeed.

"Hm-m-m," said Sergeant Madden, "we've nothing more to do right now, Willis. We'll go back to that hunk of ice you spotted comin' in, and wait for the *Aldeb*."

Patrolman Willis obediently set the hop-timer and swung the squad ship to a proper aiming. He pressed the overdrive button.

His manner, like that of Sergeant Madden, was the manner of someone conducting a perfectly routine operation.

"If my son Timmy were with me on this job," said Sergeant Madden, "I'd point out the inner meaning of the way we're going about handling it."

He reposed in his bucket-seat in the squad ship, which at that moment lay aground not quite right-side-up close to the north pole of Sirene VIII. The local sun was not in view. The squad ship's ports opened upon the incredible brilliance of the galaxy as seen out of atmosphere. There was no atmosphere here. It was all frozen. But there was a horizon, and the light of the stars showed the miniature jungle of gas crystals. Frozen gases—frozen to gas-ice—they were feathery. They were lacy. They were infinitely delicate. They were frost in three dimensions.

"Yes, sir," said Patrolman Willis.

"The *Aldeb*'s due soon," said Sergeant Madden, "so I'll make it short. The whole thing is that we are cops, and the Huks are soldiers. Which means that they're after feeling important—after glamour. Every one of 'em figures it's necessary to be important. He craves it."

Patrolman Willis listened. He had a proximity detector out, which would pick up any radiation caused by the cutting of magnetic lines of force by any object. It made very tiny whining noises from time to time. If anything from a Huk missile rocket to the salvage ship *Aldeb* approached, however, the sound would be distinctive.

"Now that," said Sergeant Madden, "is the same thing that makes delinks. A delink tries to matter in the world he lives in. It's a small world, with only him and his close pals in it. So he struts before his pals. He don't realize that anybody but him and his pals are human. See?"

"I know!" said Patrolman Willis with an edge to his voice. "Last month a couple of delinks set a ground-truck running downhill, and jumped off it, and—"

"True," said Sergeant Madden. He rumbled for a moment. "A soldier lives in a bigger world he tries to matter in. He's protectin' that world and being admired for it. In old, old days his world was maybe a day's march across. Later it got to be continents. They tried to make it planets, but it didn't work. But there've got to be enemies to protect a world against, or a soldier isn't important. He's got no glamour. Y'see?"

"Yes, sir," said Willis.

"Then there's us cops," said Sergeant Madden wryly. "Mostly we join up for the glamour. We think it's important to be a cop. But presently we find we ain't admired. Then there's no more glamour—but we're still important. A cop matters because he protects people against other people that want to do things to 'em. Against characters that want to get important by hurtin' 'em. Being a cop means you matter against all the delinks and crooks an' fools and murderers who'd pull down civilization in a minute if they could, just so they could be important because they did it. But there's no glamour! We're not admired! We just do our job. And if I sound sentimental, I mean it."

"Yes, sir," said Willis.

"There's a big picture in the big hall in Police Headquarters on Valdez III," said the sergeant. "It's the story of the cops from the early days when they wore helmets, and the days when they rode bicycles, and when they drove ground-cars. There's not only cops, but civilians, in every one of the panels, Willis. And if you look careful, you'll see that there's one civilian in every panel that's thumbin' his nose at a cop."

"I've noticed," said Willis.

"Remember it," said Sergeant Madden. "It bears on what we've got to do to handle these Huks. Soldiers couldn't do what we've got to. They'd fight, to be admired. We can't. It'd spoil our job. We've got to persuade 'em to behave themselves."

Then he frowned, as if he were dissatisfied with what he'd said. He shook his head and made an impatient gesture.

"No good," he said vexedly. "You can't say it. Hm-m-m ... I'll nap a while until the *Aldeb* gets here."

He settled back to doze.

Patrolman Willis regarded him with an odd expression. They were aground on Sirene VIII, on which no human ship had ever landed before them, and they had stirred up a hornet's nest on Sirene IV, which had orbital eighty-gee rocket missiles in orbit around it with bust bomb heads and all the other advantages of civilization. The *Aldeb* was on the way with a fifteen-man crew. And seventeen men, altogether, must pit themselves against an embattled planet with all its population ready and perhaps eager for war. Their errand was to secure the release of human prisoners and the surrender of a seized spaceship from a proud and desperate race.

It did not look promising. Sergeant Madden did not look like the kind of genius who could carry it through. Dozing, with his chin tilted forward on his chest, he looked hopelessly commonplace.

The skipper of the *Aldeb* came over to the squad ship, because Sergeant Madden loathed spacesuits and there was no air on Sirene VIII. Patrolman Willis watched as the skipper came wading through the lacy, breast-high gas-frost. It seemed a pity for such infinitely delicate and beautiful objects to be broken and crushed.

The sergeant unlocked the lock-door and spoke into a microphone when he heard the skipper stamping on the steel lock-flooring.

"Brush yourself off," commanded the sergeant, "and sweep the stuff outside. Part of its methane and there's some ammonia in those crystals."

There was a suitable pause. The outer door closed. The lock filled with air, and gas-crystal fragments turned to reeking vapor as they warmed. The skipper bled them out and refilled the lock. Then he came inside. He opened his face plate.

"Well?"

"There's Huks here," Sergeant Madden told him, "their hair in a braid and all set to go. They popped off a marker I stuck out for them to shoot at in thirty-four seconds by the clock. Bright boys, these Huks! They don't wait to ask questions. When they see something, they shoot at it."

The skipper tilted back his helmet and said beseechingly:

"Scratch my head, will you?"

When Patrolman Willis reached out his hand, the skipper revolved his head under it until the itchy place was scratched. Most men itch instantly they are unable to scratch. The skipper's space gloves were sprouting whiskers of moisture-frost now.

"Thanks," he said gratefully. "What are you going to do, sergeant?"

"Open communication with 'em," said the sergeant, heavily.

The skipper waited. Opening communication with someone who shoots on detector-contact may be difficult.

"I figure," rumbled the sergeant, "they're a lot like delinks. A cop can figure how they think, but they can't figure how a cop thinks."

"Such as?" asked the skipper.

"They can't understand anybody not tryin' to be important," said Sergeant Madden. "It baffles 'em."

"What's that got to do with the people on the *Cerberus*?" demanded the skipper. "It's our job to get them and the *Cerberus* back on the way to port!"

"I know!" conceded Sergeant Madden, "and the girl my son Timmy's going to marry is one of them. But I don't think we'll have much trouble. Have you got any multipoly plastic on the *Aldeb*?"

The skipper nodded, blankly. Multipoly plastic is a substance as anomalous as its name. It is a multiple polymer of something-or-other which stretches very accommodatingly to a surprising expanse, and then suddenly stops stretching. When it stops, it has a high and obstinate tensile strength. All ships carry it for temporary repairs, because it will seal off anything. A one-mill thickness will hold fifteen pounds pressure. Ships have been known to come down for landing with bubbles of multipoly glistening out of holes in their hulls. A salvage ship, especially, would carry an ample supply. A minor convenience in its use is the fact that a detonator-cap set off at any part of it starts a wave of disintegration which is too slow to be an explosion and cleans up the mess made in its application.

"Naturally I've got it," said the skipper. "What do you want with it?"

Sergeant Madden told him. Painfully. Painstakingly.

"The tough part," said the skipper, "is making 'em go out an ejector tube. But I've got fourteen good men. Give me two hours for the first batch. We'll make up the second while you're placing them."

Sergeant Madden nodded.

The skipper went into the lock and closed the door behind him. After a moment Patrolman Willis saw him wading through the incredibly delicate and fragile gas-ice crystals. Then the *Aldeb*'s lock swallowed him.

The odd thing about the Huk business was the minute scale of the things that happened, compared to the background in which they took place. The squad ship, for example, lifted off Sirene VIII for the second time. She'd been out once and come back for the second batch of multipoly objects. Sirene VIII was not a giant planet, by any means, but it was a respectable six thousand miles in diameter. The squad ship's sixty feet of length was a mote so minute by comparison that no comparison was possible.

She headed in toward the sun. She winked out of existence into overdrive. She headed toward Sirene IV, in quadrature, where missile rockets floated in orbit awaiting the coming of any enemy. The distance to be traveled was roughly one and a half light-hours—some twelve astronomical units of ninety-three million miles each.

The squad ship covered that distance in a negligible length of time. It popped into normality about two hundred thousand miles out from the Huk home-world. It seemed insolently to remain there. In a matter of seconds it appeared at another place—a hundred fifty thousand miles out, but off to one side. It seemed arrogantly to remain there, too—in a second place at the same time. Then it appeared, with the arbitrary effect a ship does give when coming out of overdrive, at a third place a hundred seventy-five thousand miles from the planet. At a fourth place barely eighty thousand miles short of collision with the Huk world. At a fifth place. A sixth. Each time it appeared, it seemed to remain in plain, challenging, insolent view, without ceasing to exist at the spots where it had appeared previously. In much less than a minute, the seeming of a sizable squadron of small human ships had popped out of emptiness and lay off the Huk home world at distances ranging from eighty thousand miles to three times as much.

Suddenly, light flashed intolerably in emptiness. It was in contact with one of the seeming squad ships, which ceased to be. But immediately two more ships appeared at widely different spots. A second flash—giant and terrible nearby—a pin point of light among the stars. Another ostensible human ship vanished in atomic flame—but still another appeared magically from nowhere. A third and then a fourth flash. Three more within successive seconds.

Squad ships continued to appear as if by necromancy, and space near the planet was streaked by flarings of white vapor as eighty-gee rockets hurled themselves to destruction against the invading objects. As each bomb went off, its light was brighter than the sun. But each was a mere flicker in enormousness. They flashed, and flashed—Each was a bomb turning forty kilograms of matter into pure, raw, raging destruction. Each was devastation sufficient to destroy the greatest city the galaxy ever knew.

But in that appalling emptiness they were mere scintillations. In the background of a solar system's vastness they made all the doings of men and Huks alike seem ludicrous.

For a long time—perhaps five minutes, perhaps ten—the flashings which were the most terrible of all weapons continued. Each flash destroyed something which, in scale, was less than a dust mote. But more motes appeared, and more and more and more.

And presently the flashes grew infrequent. The threads of vapor which led to each grew longer. In a little while they came from halfway around the planet. Then squad ships appeared even there. And immediately pin points of intolerable brilliance destroyed them—yet never as fast as they appeared.

Finally there came ten seconds in which no atomic flame ravened in emptiness. One more glitter. Fifteen seconds. Twenty. Thirty seconds without a flashing of atomic explosive—

The surviving objects which appeared to be squad ships hung in space. They moved without plan. They swam through space without destination. Presently the most unobservant of watches must have perceived that their movement was random. That they were not driven. That they had no purpose. That they were not squad ships but targets—and not even robot targets—set out for the missile rockets of the Huk planet to expend themselves on.

The missile rockets had expended themselves.

So Sergeant Madden opened communication with the Huks.

"These Huks," observed Sergeant Madden as the squad ship descended to the Huk planet's surface, "they must've had a share in the scrapping eighty years ago. They've got everything the old-time Huks had. They've even got recordings of human talk from civilian human prisoners of years gone by. And they kept somebody able to talk it—for when they fought with us!"

Patrolman Willis did not answer. He had a strange expression on his face. At the moment they were already within the Huk home-planet's atmosphere. From time to time a heavily accented voice gave curt instructions. It was a Huk voice, telling Patrolman Willis how to guide the squad ship to ground where—under truce—Sergeant Madden might hold conference with Huk authorities.

"*Hold the course,*" said the voice. "*That is r-right. Do as you are.*"

The horizon had ceased to be curved minutes ago. Now the ground rose gradually. The ground was green. Large green growths clustered off to one side of the flat area where the ship was to alight. They were the equivalent of trees on this planet. Undoubtedly there were equivalents of grass and shrubs, and seed-bearing and root-propagating vegetation, and Huks would make use of some seeds and roots for food. Because in order to have a civilization one has to have a larger food-supply than can be provided by even the thriftiest of grazing animals. But the Huks or their ancestors would need to have been flesh-eaters also, for brains to be useful in hunting and therefore for mental activity to be recognized as useful. A vegetarian community can maintain a civilization, but it has to start off on meat.

A clump of ground-cars waited for the squad ship's landing. The ship touched, delicately. Sergeant Madden rumbled and got out of his chair. Patrolman Willis looked at him uneasily.

"Huh!" said Sergeant Madden. "Of course you can come. You want them to think we're bluffing? No. Nothing to fight with. The Huks think our fleet's set to do the fighting."

He undogged the exit door and went out through the small vestibule which was also the ship's air lock. Patrolman Willis joined him out-of-doors. The air was fresh. The sky was blue. Clouds floated in the sky, and growing things gave off a not-unpleasant odor, and a breeze blew uncertainly. But such things happen on appropriate planets in most sol-type solar systems.

Huks came toward them. Stiffly. Defiantly. The most conspicuous difference between Huks and humans was of degree. Huks grew hair all over their heads, instead of only parts of it. But they wore garments, and some of the garments were identical and impressive, so they could be guessed to be uniforms.

"How-do," said the voice that had guided the ship down. "We are r-ready to listen to your message."

Sergeant Madden said heavily:

"We humans believe you Huks have got a good fleet. We believe you've got a good army. We know you've got good rockets and a fighting force that's worth a lot to us. We want to make a treaty for you to take over and defend as much territory as you're able to, against some characters heading this way from the Coalsack region."

Silence. The interpreter translated, and the Huks muttered astonishedly among themselves. The interpreter received instructions.

"Do you mean others of our r-race?" he demanded haughtily. "Members of our own r-race who r-return to r-recover their home worlds from humans?"

"Hell, no!" said Sergeant Madden dourly. "If you can get in contact with them and bring them back, they can have their former planets back and more besides—if they'll defend 'em. We're stretched thin. We didn't come here to fight your fleet. We came to ask it to join us."

More mutterings. The interpreter faced about.

"This surpr-rises us," he said darkly. "We know of no danger in the direction you speak of. Per-rhaps we would wish to make fr-riends with that danger instead of you!"

Sergeant Madden snorted.

"You're welcome!" Then he said sardonically: "If you're able to reach us after you try, the offer stands. Join us, and you'll give your own commands and make your own decisions. We'll co-operate with you. But you won't make friends with the characters I'm talking about! Not hardly!"

More hurried discussions still. The interpreter, defiantly: "And if we r-refuse to join you?"

Sergeant Madden shrugged.

"Nothing. You'll fight on your own, anyhow. So will we. If we joined up we could both fight better. I came to try to arrange so we'd both be stronger. We need you. You need us."

There was a pause. Patrolman Willis swallowed. At five-million-mile intervals, in a circle fifty million miles across with the Huk world as its center, objects floated in space. Patrolman Willis knew about them, because he and Sergeant Madden had put them there immediately after the missile rockets ceased to explode. He knew what they were, and his spine crawled at the thought of what would happen if the Huks found out. But the distant objects were at the limit of certain range for detection devices. The planet's instruments could just barely pick them up. They subtended so small a fraction of a thousandth of a second of arc that no information could be had about them.

But they acted like a monstrous space fleet, ready to pour down war-headed missiles in such numbers as to smother the planet in atomic flame. Patrolman Willis could not imagine admitting that such a supposed fleet needed another fleet to help it. A military man, bluffing as Sergeant Madden bluffed, would not have dared offer any terms less onerous than abject surrender. But Sergeant Madden was a cop. It was not his purpose to make anybody surrender. His job was, ultimately, to make them behave.

The Huks conferred. The conference was lengthy. The interpreter turned to Sergeant Madden and spoke with vast dignity and caginess:

"When do you r-require an answer?"

"We don't," grunted Sergeant Madden. "When you make up your minds, send a ship to Varenga III. We'll give you the information we've got. That's whether you fight with us or independent. You'll fight, once you meet these characters! We don't worry about that! Just ... we can do better together." Then he said: "Have you got the co-ordinates for Varenga? I don't know what you call it in your language."

"We have them," said the interpreter, still suspiciously.

"Right!" said Sergeant Madden. "That's all. We came here to tell you this. Let us know when you make up your minds. Now we'll go back."

He turned as if to trudge back to the squad ship. And this, of course, was the moment when the difference between a military and a cop mind was greatest. A military man, with the defenses of the planet smashed—or exhausted—and an apparent overwhelming force behind him, would have tried to get the *Cerberus* and its company turned over to him either by implied or explicit threats. Sergeant Madden did not mention them. But he had made it necessary for the Huks to do something.

They'd been shocked to numbness by the discovery that humans knew of their presence on Sirene IV. They'd been made aghast by the brisk and competent nullification of their eighty-gee rocket defenses. They'd been appalled by the appearance of a space fleet which—if it had been a space fleet—could have blasted the planet to a cinder. And then they were bewildered that the humans asked no submission—not even promises from them.

There was only one conclusion to be drawn. It was that if the humans were willing to be friendly, it would be a good idea to agree. Another idea followed. A grand gesture by Huks would be an even better idea.

"Wait!" said the interpreter. He turned. A momentary further discussion among the Huks. The interpreter turned back.

"There is a ship here," he said uneasily. "It is a human ship. There are humans in it. The ship is disabled."

Sergeant Madden affected surprise.

"Yeah? How come?"

"It ar-rived two days ago," said the interpreter. Then he plunged. "We br-rought it. We have a mine on what you call Pr-rocyron Three. The human ship landed, because it was disabled. It discovered our ship and our mine there. We wished to keep the mine secret. Because the humans had found out our secret, we br-rought them here. And the ship. It is disabled."

"Hm-m-m," said Sergeant Madden. "I'll send a repair-boat down to fix whatever's the matter with it. Of course you won't mind." He turned away, and turned back. "One of the solar systems we'd like you to take over and defend," he observed, "is Procyron. I haven't a list of the others, but when your ship comes over to Varenga it'll be ready. Talk our repair-boat down, will you? We'll appreciate anything you can do to help get the ship back out in space with its passengers, but our repair-boat can manage."

He waved his hand negligently and went back to the squad ship. He got in. Patrolman Willis followed him.

"Take her up," said Sergeant Madden.

The squad ship fell toward the sky. Sergeant Madden said satisfiedly:

"That went off pretty good. From now on it's just routine."

There was a bubble in emptiness. It was a large bubble, as such things go. It was nearly a thousand feet in diameter, and it was made of multipoly plastic which is nearly as anomalous as its name. The bubble contained almost an ounce of helium. It had a three-inch small box at one point on its surface. It floated some twenty-five million miles from the Huk planet, and five million miles from another bubble which was its identical twin. It could reflect detector-pulses. In so doing it impersonated a giant fighting ship.

Something like an hour after the squad ship rose from Sirene IV, a detonator-cap exploded in the three-inch box. It tore the box to atoms and initiated a wave of disintegration in the plastic of the bubble. The helium bubble-content escaped and was lost. The plastic itself turned to gas and disappeared.

The bubble had been capable of exactly two actions. It could reflect detector-pulses. In doing so, it had impersonated a giant fighting ship, member of an irresistible fleet. It could also destroy itself. In so doing, it impersonated a giant fighting ship—one of a fleet—going into overdrive.

In rapid succession, all the bubbles which were members of a non-existent fighting fleet winked out of existence about Sirene IV. There were a great many of them, and no trace of any remained.

The last was long gone when a small salvage ship descended to the Huk home planet. A heavily accented voice talked it down.

The salvage ship landed amid evidences of cordiality. The Huks were extremely co-operative. They even supplied materials for the repair job on the *Cerberus*, including landing rockets to be used in case of need. But they weren't needed for take-off. The *Cerberus* had been landed at a Huk spaceport, which obligingly lifted it out to space again when its drive had been replaced.

And the squad ship sped through emptiness at a not easily believable multiple of the speed of light. Sergeant Madden dozed, while Patrolman Willis performed such actions as were necessary for the progress of the ship. They were very few. But Patrolman Willis thought feverishly.

After a long time Sergeant Madden waked, and blinked, and looked benignly at Patrolman Willis.

"You'll be back with your wife soon, Willis," he said encouragingly.

"Yes, sir." Then the patrolman said explosively: "Sergeant! There's nothing coming from the Coalsack way! There's nothing for the Huks to fight!"

"True, at the moment," admitted Sergeant Madden, "but something could come. Not likely—But you see, Willis, the Huks have had armed forces for a long time. They've glamour. They're not ready to cut down and have only cops, like us humans. It wouldn't be reasonable to tell 'em the truth—that there's no need for their fighting men. They'd make a need! So they'll stand guard happily against some kind of monstrosities we'll have Special Cases invent for them. They'll stand guard zestful for years and years! Didn't they do the same against us? But now they're proud that even we humans, that they were scared of, ask them to help us. So presently they'll send some Huks over to go through the Police Academy, and then presently there'll be a sub-precinct station over there, with Huks in charge, and ... why ... that'll be that."

"But they want planets—"

Sergeant Madden shrugged.

"There's plenty, Willis. The guess is six thousand million planets fit for humans in this galaxy. And by the time we've used them up, somebody'll have worked out a drive to take us to the next galaxy to start all over. There's no need to worry about that! And for immediate—does it occur to you how many men are going to start getting rich because there's a brand-new planet that's got a lot of things we humans would like to have, and wants to buy a lot of things the Huks haven't got?"

Patrolman Willis subsided. But presently he said:

"Sergeant ... what'd you have done if they hadn't told you about the *Cerberus*?"

Sergeant Madden snorted.

"It's unthinkable! We waltzed in there, and told them a tale, and showed every sign of walkin' right out again without askin' them a thing. They couldn't even tell us to go to hell, because it looked like we didn't care what they said. It was insupportable, Willis! Characters that make trouble, Willis, do it to feel important. And we'd left them without a thing to tell us that was important enough to mention—unless they told us about the *Cerberus*. We had 'em baffled. They needed to say something, and that was the only thing they could say!"

He yawned.

"The *Aldeb* reports everybody on the *Cerberus* safe and sound, only frightened, and the skipper said Timmy's girl was less scared than most. I'm pleased. Timmy's getting married, and I wouldn't want my grandchildren to have a scary mother!"

He looked at the squad ship's instruments. There was a long way yet to travel.

"A-h-h-h! It's a dull business this, overdrive," he said somnolently. "And it's amazing how much a man can sleep when everything's in hand, and there's nothing ahead but a wedding and a few things like that. Just routine, Willis. Just routine!"

He settled himself more comfortably as the squad ship went on home.

THE END

CPSIA information can be obtained
at www.ICGtesting.com
Printed in the USA
LVHW041022020323
740706LV00008B/1125